STATE FLOWERS OF THE USA

For Students and Teachers

Enjoy learning about the State Flowers of the USA and coloring them!

Alabama

Camellia

ALASKA

Forget Me Not

ARIZONA

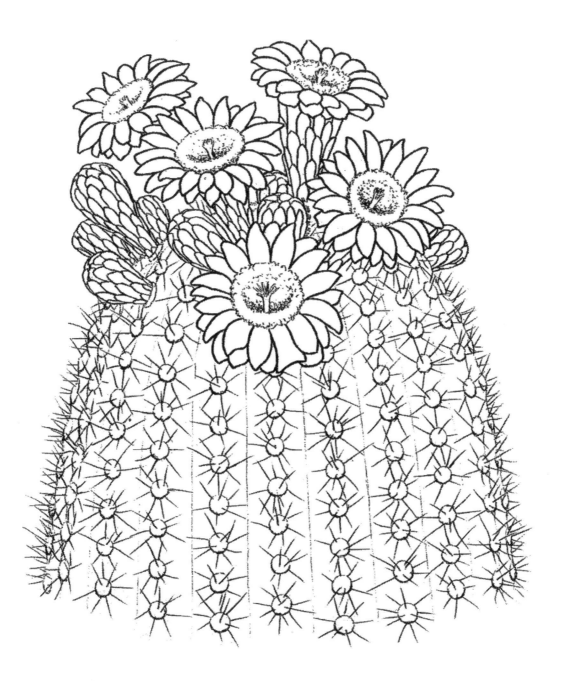

Saguaro Cactus Blossom

ARKANSAS

Apple Blossom

California

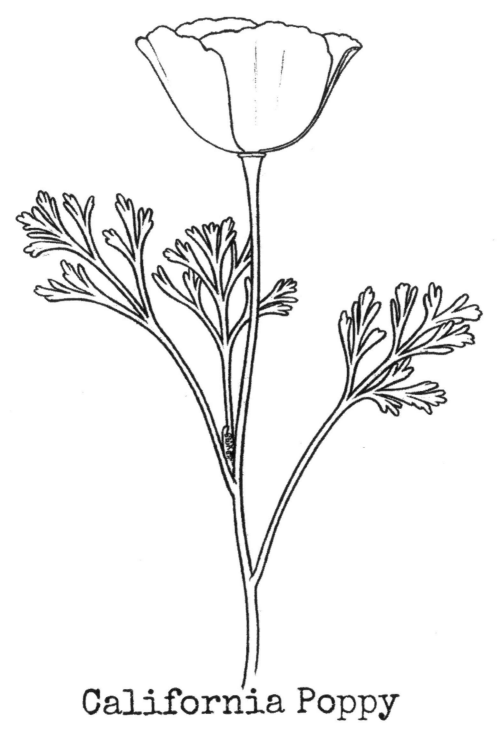

California Poppy

COLORADO

Rocky Mountain
Columbine

Connecticut

Mountain Laurel

DELAWARE

Peach Blossom

FLORIDA

Orange Blossom

GEORGIA

Cherokee Rose

Hawaii

Hibiscus

IDAHO

Syringa

Illinois

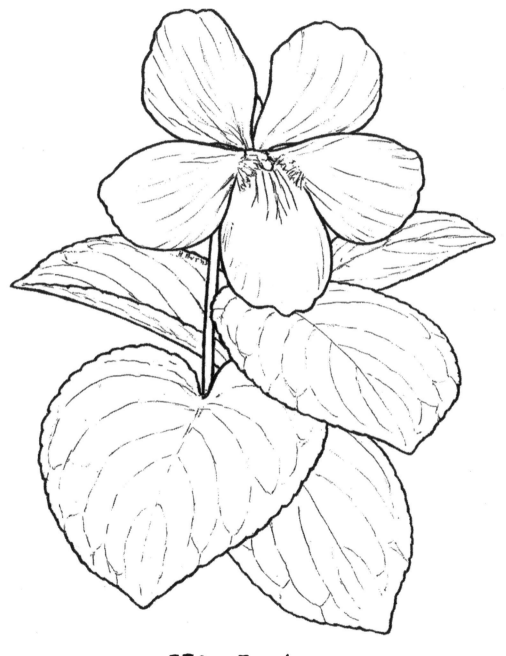

Violet

Indiana

Peony

Iowa

Wild Prairie Rose

Kansas

Sunflower

Kentucky

Goldenrod

Louisiana

Magnolia

MAINE

White Pine Cone

MARYLAND

Blackeyed Susan

MASSACHUSETTS

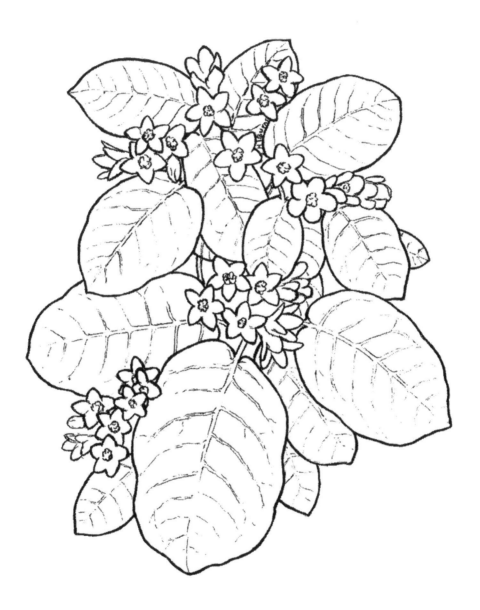

Mayflower

Michigan

Apple Blossom

MINNESOTA

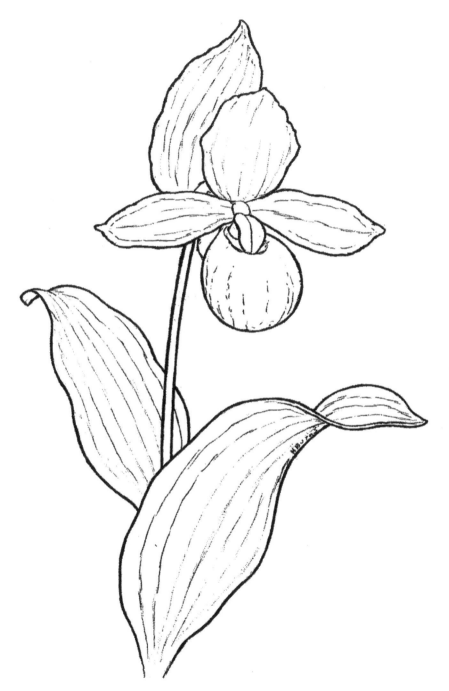

Pink & White Lady Slipper

MISSISSIPPI

Magnolia

MISSOURI

White Hawthorn Blossom

Montana

Bitterroot

NEBRASKA

Goldenrod

NEVADA

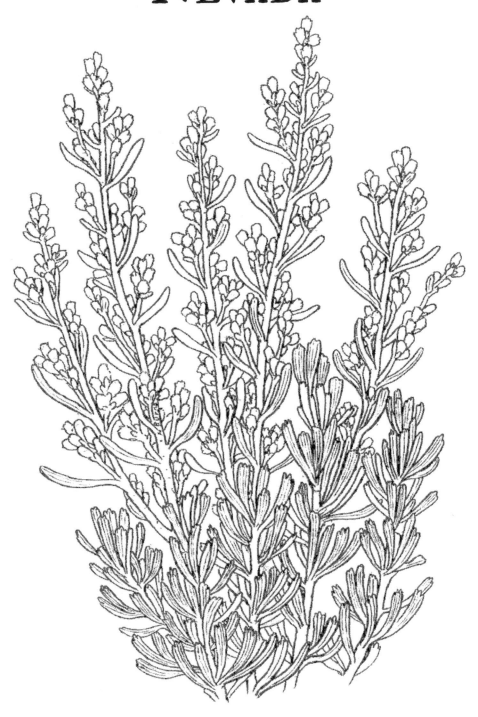

Sagebrush

New Hampshire

Purple Lilac

NEW JERSEY

Violet

New Mexico

Yucca Flower

NEW YORK

Rose

NORTH CAROLINA

Dogwood

North Dakota

Prairie Rose

OHIO

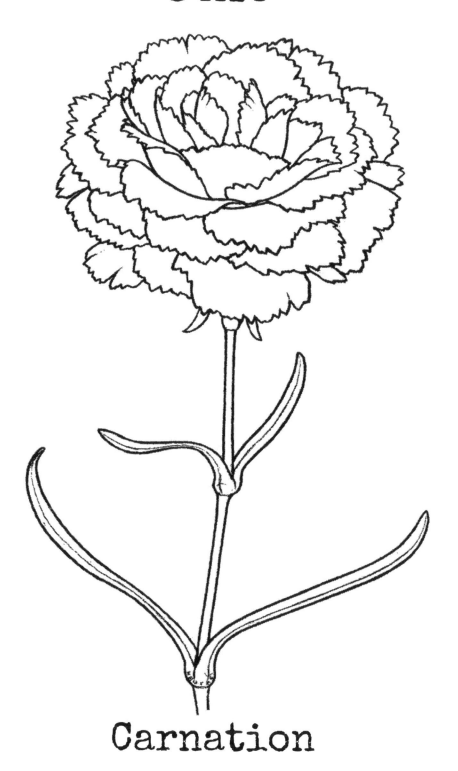

Carnation

OKLAHOMA

Rose

OREGON

Oregon Grape

PENNSYLVANIA

Mountain Laurel

RHODE ISLAND

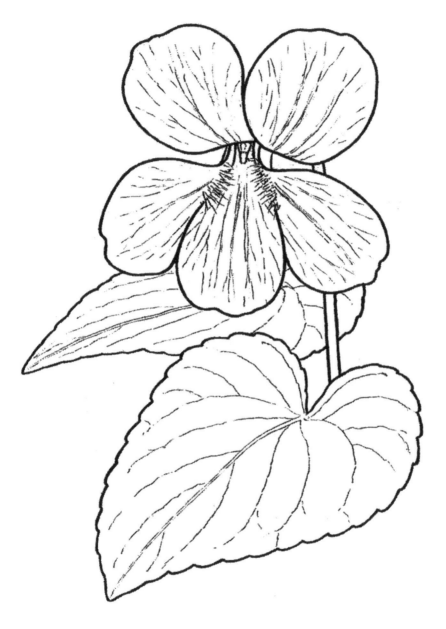

Violet

SOUTH CAROLINA

Yellow Jessamine

SOUTH DAKOTA

Pasque Flower

Tennessee

Iris

Texas

Bluebonnet

Utah

Sego Lily

Vermont

Red Clover

VIRGINIA

American Dogwood

Washington

Rhododendron

WEST VIRGINIA

Rhododendron

WISCONSIN

Wood Violet

Wyoming

Indian Paintbrush

41466013R00059

Made in the USA
San Bernardino, CA
13 November 2016